Reflections of My Life

by Paul Kuypers

ISBN 978-1-64663-181-0

Published by

köehlerbooks™

3705 Shore Drive
Virginia Beach, VA 23455
800-435-4811
www.koehlerbooks.com

REFLECTIONS *of My Life*

PAUL KUYPERS

VIRGINIA BEACH
CAPE CHARLES

TABLE OF CONTENTS

INTRODUCTION

THE STORY YOU ARE ABOUT to read is my story. It's a true story full of pain and sadness, happiness, laughter and even miracles.

My name is Paul Kuypers. I am just an ordinary guy who decided to start writing books. Although this is my very first real book, I did write a collection of quotes and sayings called *Healing Messages from Above.*

Although I started writing, I don't see myself as an author. I see myself more as somebody who found a new passion. The passion for writing is still very new to me, and maybe I won't even continue doing it.

But I wanted to tell you my story . . . the story of my life. I may still be young with few life experiences, but I'm sure I have plenty more to come. On the other hand, as you read my story you may feel like I have already had a life full of experiences.

In this book I will take you on a journey through my life starting from my childhood to present day. At times I go from present back to events that happened to me years ago. I have mentioned certain names in this book with permission. I have left out certain names to protect myself and members of my family, who might have issues dealing with some of the experiences we endured together.

However concerning some chapters may be, I can tell you they're not all like that. Though it was hard to write certain chapters, I feel I have written them with honesty and integrity. I started and stopped many times because I did not want to hurt any family members, especially my sisters, who went through many of the same things I did.

I told one of my sisters about my idea of writing my story. When she read the first few lines of a specific chapter, she cried. Her reaction put doubts in my mind about continuing with the book. But she encouraged me to keep writing. Her reaction finally helped me decide to keep telling my story.

CHAPTER 1
IN THE BEGINNING

Life should be carefree, not a living nightmare.

I WAS BORN ON THE nineteenth of November. On the day of my birth, my mother was twenty-nine years old. She was already bringing up five young daughters. I was her wish come true. She always wanted a boy. Growing up with five older sisters, I was spoiled with lots of attention. Although things were rough, I had the love from my mother and sisters.

I never knew my father. He was never in my life. I have been told a few things about him. Apparently, he had the same name as me and was Italian. My mother always said that I could look for him if I wanted, but I never felt the urge to do so. Why would I look for someone who did not want me in the first place? I do sometimes think about him when I see commercials on TV of sons with their dads. Sometimes I get sad. Other times they have no effect at all. Either way, I don't have the need to look for him. I am doing fine with just having my mother in my life.

How my mother managed to provide for the six of us was a miracle. We did not have a lot of money and at times had to get by with very little. Sometimes we had to steal fruit from big trolleys that the shops put outside, and, yes, we also borrowed money to survive the rest of the month. At times my mother could not give back the money she borrowed by the due date, but most of the time she did. She was a single parent on a low income. Every penny she got was spent on us or on getting us food. She provided the best she could.

We lived in a quiet neighborhood, and at the end of our street lived my best friend at that time. We became friends going to the same school, which was located just meters away from our houses. We were also in the same class.

My friend and I spend a lot of time together, not only in school but also outside school. I was so lucky not only to have him as a friend, but also to have him as my neighbor. Despite having other friends we spent time with, we spent most of the time together. Everything was fine for a long time, but that soon changed.

But it was not our friendship that changed. (At least not yet.)

At one point, my family had a lovely man in our life called Sheriff. Although I don't remember him, I have been told many stories about him. He loved us all, but I heard that I was sort of his favorite. Sometimes he would let us do things that my mother would not allow, like sitting on a motorbike. I wish I could remember him, but unfortunately, I don't. I have a photo of him, so I know what he looked like, but that's where it stops, at least for me. My sisters are luckier and do remember him. He was a good friend to my mother and to us.

However, Sheriff went on regular holidays, and once, when he stayed away longer than usual, another person came into our lives. I don't remember how he came into our lives, and really, I don't want to know.

Calling him a person is not accurate, though. I would call him a horrible monster. The reason? He made our life a living hell, and the one who suffered the most was our mother. Any little thing he did not like caused him to become violent. It did not matter what it was; he would start throwing objects and furniture around, and he would beat her.

Even when Sheriff returned, that monster was there hiding behind the front door, signaling to my mum to send him away, and, of course, when he left and she closed the door . . . well, you can imagine.

I guess he was too scared to fight a real man. Instead, he took it out on my mother and us. When he had one of his episodes, my sisters and I always hid in a corner of another room. Because my sisters were older than me, they knew what was happening. I was still very young and did not understand. One time, I cried, of course, and called for my mother.

He came to the room where we were hiding and smashed things up in there. To make sure that it did not happen again, and to make things easier for my mother, one of my sisters would add a little alcohol in my drink bottle so I would fall asleep and be quiet during his rages. I totally understand now why she did that, and I am grateful.

Every day, this monster, who I can't call a man, was violent and threatened us.

One time he even put a knife to my mother's throat. And since we were still kids, we were not able to do much. This continued for about eight long years. During those years, we stayed in safe houses and went for help to the fire department where we explained everything. The police escorted us back home, and the moment the monster arrived in the house, they took him away. As I was still very young, I don't remember everything that happened after that. My next memory is of moving, and I didn't get the chance to say goodbye to my best friend.

We moved to a smaller house, but that is not where the story of the monster ends. Somehow, he managed to find us again, and the same thing started all over again. I remember that one day I sensed that he was going to be violent again, so I made the excuse of going to play outside. While I was outside, I saw him through the window throwing a table over and tossing other things around. I ran as fast as I could to my sister's house to tell her what was happening. After that, everything is a bit of blur for me, apart from knowing that she came back with me.

The next thing I remember is moving to Den Helder, where my sister lived, for a while, and even there, he found us. There he forced my mother to cash out paychecks and give the money to him. One of my sisters told my mother that she should not take it anymore, and that she should leave and go with her.

At first my mother refused, but my sister said, "Please, Mom, come with me before it's too late."

My mother agreed. "Yes, we'll all go together." And we left. All I remember is that we went back to live in Amsterdam, and that monster of a man was not part of our lives anymore. I had to grow up quickly, and missed out on having a childhood. He took that away from me.

CHAPTER 2
WHEN FRIENDSHIP ENDS

Friends don't always stay friends. Sometimes you lose them.

AS I NOW WAS A bit older, I decided to try to get in contact with my best friend.

Luckily for me, he still had his old phone number, so we made a plan to meet up.

The day that we met up, I walked once again through our old neighborhood where he still lived. It was a cold and weird feeling. Remembering what happened all those years ago did not make it any better. Horrible memories filled my mind again, but not for too long.

The sky was grey, and the air smelled funny. For one moment when I was close to our old street I doubted whether I could walk into the street, but I was brave, and the thought of seeing my old friend got me through it. When I saw my friend again, it felt weird but at the same time so familiar. We spent the day together and caught up with each other's lives. It was like old times, remembering things we did in our childhood, like climbing into trees and throwing fruit at people's windows and then hiding in the trees so they did not see us.

He seemed a bit different, but as it was nice to see him again after such a long time, I did not pay too much attention to it. After our first reunion, I did not want to lose our friendship again. I finally had my friend back, and that meant a lot to me. I was not planning to let him go again.

So, after a couple days I called him again and arranged another day to see each other.

When we met for the second time, things were different. He was still in bed when I arrived. Not only that, but he also looked stoned, or was stoned. Despite that, we had a nice day together, although it was inside, and he spent most of the time in bed.

When the day ended and I was about to go home, I told him that it was time for him to contact me—when he could, of course. He said he would, but that never happened. He never called me or tried any other form of contacting me. Suddenly my old best friend was not there anymore. I could have called him myself, but I felt that he did not care much about our friendship anymore. Maybe other things were now more important for him.

That is not the way I would like to think back on him. Despite all of it, I am grateful to him for being there for me and for being a part of my life. During the horrible years my family went through, he was there for me and gave me the distraction I needed.

I know friends come and go, but he was my very first best friend. That is why it really hurt me deeply. He was my best friend, and then it was suddenly over. I was hurt, and this made me not want to have friends anymore. I did not want to go through the bloody same thing again—to have my trust be damaged again. No . . . not again.

It was not till much later I met someone who showed me that true friendship still was possible. He restored that trust again in me.

CHAPTER 3
LEAVING MOTHER'S NEST

Moving out is never easy but sometimes necessary.

IN MY TEENAGE YEARS, I still lived at home with my mother and my youngest sister.

I would go out on the weekends to a local bar down the street, normally with my two other sisters and my brother-in-law. As we went almost every weekend, we became friends with others who also went there every weekend.

We quickly became known as the people who got the party started. Probably because we always danced when the music was playing, or we sang out loud, and when we did everybody else joined in. We were even, at one point, given the name "party makers." We got jumpers made with the name *Party Makers* on them, which we always wore when we went out.

As a group we did a lot together, like spending a day at the beach or going out for a meal, etc. As I was still reasonably young, my mother did not like it and did not want me to hang out with them anymore. I retaliated against her, which is what you would expect, really, from anyone my age.

Arguments happened more and more frequently with my mother. It didn't make me lose respect for her. We just could not get along anymore.

Now, years later, of course I do understand her and know that she was trying to protect me, and I don't blame her for reacting that way.

But back then everything was different. I was a teenager, nearly an adult, and did not understand it. Why could I not enjoy myself and have a nice time? At one point it got so bad that I asked my sister if I could live with her as it was impossible for me to live at home.

Luckily, she agreed to it, and when I told my mother she was not happy, but I had made my choice, and as soon as I could move, I moved in with my sister. Unfortunately, my mother also got angry with her, and we lost contact with her for about a year or so.

Living with my sister was great. I had a job, and we shared the household and I paid her rent money.

We had the best and sometimes the greatest of times together, like watching very late TV. She would fall asleep during the movie, and when I went to switch the TV off, she always woke up and said, "Hey, I am still watching!" So, I had to put the TV back on so she could watch again until she fell asleep again. This would continue at least three times before I could finally switch it off. She still does this today. It makes me laugh just thinking about it.

On the weekends, there was a kids' program early in the morning, and because we liked the early-morning song, we got up early every weekend to watch it and sing out loud. And we loved buying warm maize bread from the bakery, which we always ate on our way back home.

At one point we both talked about moving to a new house. She wanted to move, and I wanted to have a house of my own as well. I remember wanting a downstairs house with a garden, close to the shops. Yes, I know I was asking for a lot, but funnily enough, when I was selected to view the house, I got exactly what I wanted.

And a week after hearing that I had the house, my sister got the news that she was moving too. We moved to our new houses at the same time, and helped each other with our stuff.

I loved living on my own. I was my own boss now and decided what I wanted to do and when.

The only thing that was difficult in the beginning was deciding where I wanted everything placed; that was up to me now. For the rest, everything sorted itself out.

I did not want to buy pictures to hang on my walls. Instead, I wanted to have my own drawings that I made or copied. I was very proud of them and wanted to show them off, I guess.

I really enjoyed having my own place, but after living there for about two years, things started to change. It was not really that I did not enjoy it there anymore; I really did. But every time I came home from work, I had people over at my place. In the beginning, it was fine, but when it started to happen more and more, I started to hate it. People just wanted to drop by as if it were nothing.

So, I informed everybody from the family to please call if they wanted to come by to see me.

Don't get me wrong; I love my family, but sometimes I was tired after work and just did not want to have any visitors. I wanted to relax and do my own things, like watch TV or just have a nap. Why not? It was my house, my rules.

They might not have liked it straightaway when I told them that, but in the end they did understand it and respected my wishes. After that, everything was fine, and I enjoyed the rest of my time living there. Until I left Amsterdam to live abroad.

CHAPTER 4
A NEW BEST FRIEND

True friendships are hard to find but still exist.

WHEN I STARTED MY SECOND job, I met Dirk, not knowing that he would become my new best friend. And he still is.

It was a day like every other day. I worked behind the machine with a few other colleagues, and we were just having normal conversation. When having a break, we started talking about a TV program that we had heard of. We were laughing about the name of the TV program, or rather the name we gave it. At that point, Dirk and I started to have that connection.

From that day onwards, we talked every day, but as I had decided previously, I did not want to get close with anybody to become friends again. Not after what happened with my old best friend. So, although I had contact with Dirk at work, I otherwise kept my distance.

As weeks went by, the friendship between Dirk and I kept growing. I even talked with his sister and brother, without seeing them. The day that he invited me to his home to meet them, he warned me his sister would be waiting with the rolling pin, and his brother would send his dog at me.

I can tell you that's exactly what happened. Of course, it was all fun and games, and the dog was lovely.

We became very close friends, so there was nothing else I could do but surrender.

I also became friends with a friend of his called Rick. I had met him once and asked him what his name was. When he answered in a strong voice, it took me a bit by surprise, and I left him alone after that.

It was not until Dirk really introduced him to me that we formed a bond. Now I see him as a big soft teddy bear as he is a lovely person. I am glad to have him as a friend. In the meantime, the friendship between Dirk and me became stronger and stronger.

We started to see each other more and more out of work, just going into the city together or going out at night till the early morning. We were able to talk about everything, and we even finished each other's sentences at one point. From there we started to give each other presents and exchanged them at work by the lockers before our workday began or during a break.

Now, in the time that I became friends with Dirk, there was another colleague who was already friends with him. I sort of became friends with him as well but did not have the connection that I had with Dirk and Rick.

The funny part about it was that they had a good friendship before I started to work there. But when my friendship became stronger with Dirk, he fell a bit to the background. I always said that I was an obstacle between him and Dirk. And Dirk always said that he did not see it that way, but we had some good laughs at this other guy's expense.

We had some great moments at work. Once, Rick tied me to a trolley so well that I was unable to free myself. I asked Dirk to help me, but of course he had too much fun seeing me struggle to get loose and refused to help me. It was not until one of the bosses came by and asked what was going on that I was freed.

There are so many memories that it is just impossible to mention them all. We still have and create great moments when I am over in Amsterdam that will make great memories for times to come. Apart from the great times, we also had our more serious moments, and the best thing was that we were able to tell each other everything.

He was the first person I told that I was gay.

Thanks to Dirk, I started to believe I could let people in my life again and even become friends with them.

Without knowing, Dirk gave me my trust back. He showed me that true friendship still existed.

With that said, I want to close this chapter with a little something I wrote for him.

> My dear friend, when I first got to know you, I kept my distance. When time went by, things changed, but I still did not let you into my life. You see, my dear friend, I have been there and trusted someone to be my friend. In the end it was nothing more than me fooling myself. I was hurt and could not trust or let anybody come close to me again. But you, my dear friend, showed me that true friendship still exists. Thanks to you I have made more friends, friends that I never thought I would let in. I keep my distance sometimes—I still do. My dear friend, I have many friends now who care about me and most of all love me for who I am. My dear friend, thank you for what you have given me. Although my friendship circle has grown, there will never be a friend like you.

CHAPTER 5
COMING OUT

Coming out is hard enough.
Finding out you're gay is a whole other thing.

THEY SAY COMING OUT IS sometimes easy and sometimes very hard to do. But what if you don't even know that you are gay, lesbian or transsexual? What if you always thought you were straight? Well, that happened to me.

I always assumed that I was straight and never thought any different. I was infatuated with girls in middle school and had my heart broken a few times. In my late teens, I fell in love with a woman who I met at a bus stop on my way to work. We were friends for a long time, but I did not have the heart to tell her how deeply I felt for her. So, I stayed friends in the beginning, but as time passed by, my feelings for her became stronger and eventually became love.

At that time, she was in a relationship with someone else, but as she did not know I liked her in that way, I kept quiet and stayed her friend. It was not until their relationship ended that I opened up to her, and soon after we started a relationship.

The relationship did not last long—less than a couple of months. And no, our relationship did not end because I found out I was gay. At that point, as far as I was aware, I was straight. Our relationship ended because she was a jealous person and thought I was spending more time with others than her. Which was not true. I wanted to be with her but could not deal with her jealousy.

Now I was single again. I could do whatever I wanted and had nobody to tell what I was doing or going to do.

It was in that time that I started to realize that I was gay.

One day, I walked past a guy. I remember looking at him and thinking that he was good looking. This happened a couple of times, and then I started to feel more attracted to men than women. And every time I saw a man who looked nice, those feelings came back to me. I told myself not to be so stupid because I liked women, not men. I told myself that a lot.

One day I thought about why I had those feelings for men and felt the attraction to them. I came to the only conclusion: I was most probably gay.

Even at this point, I was not sure. So, the only way for me to find out was to try it out with a man. But how was I going to do that? How would I make a connection with someone?

I started by first looking on the world wide web and joining some gay chat groups. But all I found there were people who I would probably never meet or have a sexual experience with. In the end it did not help me at all, but I must admit the attention that I got gave me a good feeling.

Around this time, I met a guy at work who was gay, and he told me he suspected that I was gay too. I pretended that I was not and that he was wrong. At that point I was still finding out myself how I felt and was not sure yet. But that talk made me more curious, and after a week or so I admitted that I was having strong feelings for men.

He told me that he liked me, and I started to like him too. So, during one of our work breaks we decided to go out together and, well, let's say play with each other.

When break time came, we stepped into his car and we drove off. I had no clue where he was taking me, but at that moment I did not really care. We stopped by an abandoned road and went into some bushes where we basically only touched each other and nothing more. Not even kissing. It just stayed at touching. That was it, and we returned to work.

I don't remember how I felt after that, but we decided that the next time we would take it further. I remember that time at my house very well. It was on my nephew's birthday. I was off that day and could not help but think about what was going to happen that evening. I thought about it all day! When he arrived, there was no coffee, no small talk; we basically got the ball rolling. I was so nervous. I did not know what to do but did what I thought was right. That was the very first time I had sex with a man. I can't call it making love as I was not in love with him, but I needed the experience in order to confirm my sexuality.

Later that evening, when it was all over and he was gone, I went to my nephew's birthday but could not really focus on what was happening. All I could think about was what happened, and I realized from that moment on that I liked men more than women.

Now that I knew I was gay, I decided to wait a while before telling my family. Not because I was ashamed of it, but because I had just realized myself that I was gay. I had to come to terms with it.

And why should I have to tell my family? My love life was none of their business, but if they asked me, I would of course tell them—although apparently they already knew. But the first person I really told about what happened was my best friend, Dirk, who understood me and did not judge me for being who I was.

CHAPTER 6
MOROCCO

Getting lost in a strange country is not the best thing to do.

GOING ON A HOLIDAY WAS never possible for me. Not until I was older and had money to do so. Before I tell you about my very first holiday alone, I would like to tell you about another holiday I went on.

My first holiday was not alone. I was invited to go to Morocco with a colleague of mine, who had a house there, for three weeks. He went every summer and asked me if I wanted to go with him and his family.

As I had never been on holiday before, it was very tempting to go, but I was not sure and a bit scared about going on my own with him and his family. I asked another colleague of mine if she wanted to go with me, and luckily for me, she said yes.

The day of the holiday, we met at a station where we would take the coach to Spain and from there take the ferry to Tangiers where he had his house. The route would be from Amsterdam to Belgium, to France, and then into Spain.

The journey to Spain was a nightmare. The coach stopped at different places to collect people and stopped every four hours for like ten to fifteen minutes so they could change drivers, who took turns bringing us to our destination. That was the only good thing about it because I could stretch my legs and get some fresh air; the smell in the coach was not pleasant at all.

I did manage to sleep off and on during the journey, but it was uncomfortable. It was a very long trip, but finally by day three we made it to Algeciras in Spain to get the ferry.

Once on the ferry, I had time to enjoy the beautiful surroundings. While crossing from Spain to Tangiers, I noticed in the distance an island and thought that it looked nice, so I took a picture of it, not knowing that I would five years later meet my husband there.

When we arrived in Tangiers and at my colleague's house, the holiday finally could begin. As my female colleague and I had never been there, we did not know where to go, and we always went out with his family or with him alone. There was so much to see and do, but we never had time enough as we had to go back for lunch, snack or dinner.

It was apparently normal for them to eat three or four times a day there, and you all ate from one big dish and had your own portions of food. You did not touch the other person's portion as that was considered rude or even an insult suggesting that you had not eaten enough.

This was all okay. I've always adjusted to traditions of other countries. But then it started to get boring; you had to eat while you were not even hungry or still full of the last meal.

What also became boring was always having to go out with him or the whole family. We just wanted to go by ourselves, which they were not happy about. After talking to my colleague about going out on our own, we decided we would do exactly that. So, on our last outing with him we took extra care to note the route there and back.

On the day that we went alone, we had a great time. We did not rush to go back for lunch or whatever, and did what we wanted. When we did go back, we stepped into a taxi and gave the taxi driver the name of the bank we'd written on a piece of paper so we would remember the name. The bank was close to my colleague's house and a good landmark.

Little did we know there were a lot of banks with the same name. Apparently if you just say the bank's name, they take you to the main bank in the town. So, when he dropped us off there, we straightaway knew that it was the wrong place. But as we were not able to communicate with the driver, we got out and, yes, we were lost. We didn't really know what to do and tried to find someone who could speak English and see if something looked familiar to us. Luckily for us, we found a man who was able to help us. He took us in his car to the correct place. To this day I am very grateful to this man who went out of his way to help us.

Off course, my colleague was not impressed with us for getting lost, and I can understand that he was worried, but we still decided to go on our own to town after going one last time with him. We never got lost again and had a good time the rest of the holiday. The only thing I was not looking forward to was the three-day drive back to Amsterdam in that coach.

The year after, I went on a holiday on my own.

CHAPTER 7
A HOLIDAY ALONE

I met you at the right time. I was not alone.

I HAD MY HEART SET on going to Greece as I always wanted to go there to see the historical monuments, etc.

But it turned out to be expensive, and that was money I did not have at the time. So, I was a bit disappointed and had to look for another holiday destination.

Somebody mentioned Turkey to me, and my first reaction was "no thank you." But after thinking about it and looking at some places over there, I decided, in the end, to go. I would go to Kusadasi, a famous tourist place.

I was scared. I was going alone, to Turkey of all places. And I was going for two weeks.

But I needed to do this—maybe just to prove something to myself. Who knows.

My family came with me to the airport to say goodbye. When it was time to go, I said one more goodbye before going to the gate.

I had a good flight, and when we landed it had already started to get dark. I collected my bag and headed to the exit where I was picked up by the airport pickup, which drove me to the hotel. While checking me in, the man at the front desk asked me if I had eaten something. I replied that I hadn't.

He gave me a sandwich wrapped in cling film. I took it from him and thanked him. After that I went up to check out my room, ate the sandwich, and then called the family, saying I arrived safely, before turning in for the night.

The next day I went down for breakfast and then went back upstairs to get myself sorted for the day. I wondered what to do on my first full day in a strange country all by myself. In the end I stayed inside the hotel and my hotel room.

That evening I realized that I had just wasted a day of my holiday and went to sleep.

The next morning, I was determined to go out, so when I stood on my balcony, I looked at the harbor and decided to have a look around there. Well, I went and walked the whole harbor before again returning to my hotel.

I remember thinking, *Well, you screwed another day up. What a bloody idiot you are. You're here on holiday and just walked around the harbor doing nothing basically.* I decided there and then that I could not waste more days like that and that I would go to the center of town tomorrow. When morning broke, I got out and went to the town center to have a look around and maybe even buy something I would like—if not, then postcards to send to my family back in Amsterdam.

Walking around in town, I looked at the souvenir shops and bought some postcards. I passed by an excursion place where I was stopped by a man holding flyers. He of course tried to get me to do an excursion and gave me one of the flyers.

The only thing I was thinking at that moment was *I must get out of here*, but he did not let me go so quickly. He asked where I came from and what my name was.

After telling him where I came from and my name, he said that his name was Yilmaz. He started to talk to me in Flemish and told me that he had lived in Belgium for a long time. It was nice to hear somebody speaking in Dutch or Flemish, but I still wanted to get out of there. Before I left, he told me that not only should I come to book an excursion but that I also could come by and sit with him and talk. Which seemed strange to me, but I let that thought go.

When he finally let me go, I continued my day but made sure that on my way back I walked on the other side of the street so I did not have to pass him again.

That evening in my room I thought about him and looked through the brochure with excursions in it. As I needed to get out and enjoy my holiday, I went back the next day to that excursion office and booked my first excursion with him.

The excursion was to Effes, a place in Turkey full of historical monuments and buildings, which I loved.

After booking my first excursion with him, or really the excursion place he worked for, I went basically every day to see him, either to book an excursion or just to hang out with him while he was working. Together we went to Bodrum, Pamukale and a few other places.

On one of the excursions there was a problem with the seating; apparently there was not enough space for everybody, but there was a space in the very back where you could put your shopping or whatever. I think you can say that it was a sort of boot. So, because there was no space, he asked me if I would not mind sitting there so the other tourists would not complain about it. I said yes, and as a joke I said, "But you must buy me two beers," which he did.

He also made sure he was sitting at the back row so he could keep an eye on me. Maybe he thought I was uncomfortable, but, to be honest, I was okay sitting there with my two beers. Okay, I could not see anything until we were at the destination, but that was the only issue.

During the drive there he held my hand as well. Why he did that I still don't know. Maybe, like I said, he was worried about me, but it was nice anyway that he cared.

The days that I did not go on an excursion, I just stayed with him at the excursion place and spent time with him and even had lunch together. We talked about everything, and as we got to know each other better, we also talked about sex.

I can't recall if I told him that I was gay. I think I didn't, but he said he liked men and women, which I of course had no problem with.

I think from that day I started to get feelings for him but never really told him. I also became friends with his friends, and even with the guy who owned a jewelry shop next door.

I remember going into that shop and looking at a golden chain that I liked. When I asked the guy how much it was and he told me the price, I told him that I would like to buy it but had to come back later that day as I did not have that money on me. What he told me next stunned me. He said that I could have it now and just come back later to pay it. So, I walked out of there with a golden chain without paying. Of course, later that day I paid him the money.

Then the time came to say goodbye to my Turkish friend Yilmaz. At the end of my holiday, he arranged for me to be brought to the airport. Before I left, he told me to come back next month.

I said to him, "Are you crazy? I can't afford that." He said to try to come anyway, and I just said I would, although it would be impossible.

When we said our final goodbye, he gave me a kiss on the cheek, and I got in the car and gave him a wave before driving off. Back in Amsterdam I kept in contact with him. He had given me his mobile number and the number of the excursion place. The thought of going back the next month was very tempting, but I just could not do it.

I did manage to go the month after, but only for a week. When I told him, he was very happy to hear that I was coming again. He told me to only buy the plane ticket, and he would arrange the hotel for me. Not only that, but he said that he would pick me up from the airport, which was nice as I didn't have to wait to see him.

When I arrived at the airport, he was there as promised to pick me up. I gave him a hug, and then we walked together to the car. We stopped at the place where he worked, and I said hello to all the other friends that I made in the excursion place and outside it. After that we walked to the hotel where I would stay for the week.

I could not believe what he had arranged for me. I was staying in a hotel that was run by a Dutch family. He let me settle in, and I would meet up with him later. For now he had to go back to work.

Staying in the hotel with the Dutch family was great, and before I knew it, we became friends as well. I even had breakfast with them instead of having it at the breakfast area. And in the evenings, we always stayed up late and had the best conversations. During one of our many conversations, they learned that I did tarot readings, and they were very into that. The daughter of the family even bought some tarot cards so I could do tarot readings for all of them and teach her to do readings.

I ended up doing some for other people there, but for one person who wanted a reading I could not follow through, meaning that I could not finish the reading. I just got a bad feeling about him; my body shook. I did not want to continue and said that I could not see anything else for him. Later, when he was gone, I told the family about how I felt during the reading, and they confirmed he was not a good person.

In the end, I had a great week with them, as I did with Yilmaz, who, of course, I spent the most time with. One day I was with him in the afternoon, but he was so busy that I decided to go back to the hotel and let him do his job. I told his friend to let him know that I went back to the hotel and that I would return later. Well, was I in for a surprise; later that day he came to pick me up from the hotel, and when we were walking back to his work, he told me off—not in a bad way, but in a concerned way, saying that I should not have left without letting him know. He grew worried when he did not see me when he came back out from the office. I understood his worry and promised not to do it anymore. Being with him was the best. Although it was just for a week, it felt like I was there much longer.

At the end of the week, he brought me back to the airport, and before we said goodbye, he told me that the next time I came, I would stay with him.

The year after, I decided to go with my sister, her son, and a friend of ours to Turkey.

While planning the holiday, I already knew where I was going to stay. I just needed to sort out where my family would stay. I could not wait to tell Yilmaz about me coming over with my family but was more excited that this time I would stay at his place.

When I finally called him on his mobile to tell him the news, there was no answer, which was strange. He always answered it, but this time he didn't. I thought nothing of it, and I called the office where he worked. A friend of his who I had become friends with as well picked up the phone. We had some small talk, but when I asked to speak to Yilmaz, well . . . I could not believe the words that followed from the other side of the phone.

"Yilmaz died" were the words that came like a bombshell. My friend explained what happened, but I was in such shock that I was not really listening. I just remember feeling numb, and it took me a while to answer my friend, who was asking if I was still there.

With a dry mouth I explained that we were coming to Turkey on holiday. My friend said he was very happy and was hoping to see us soon.

When I hung up the phone, I told my sister, who was there with me, that he had died, and then just broke down and cried.

What had happened was that Yilmaz had something to drink and then had to do something, so he decided to get on a bike and do what had to be done. He then saw a dolmus bus, as they call it there, coming towards him, and he tried to swerve around it, but while swerving, he slipped and hit his head against the front of the bus. I heard he was killed instantly. I was, for a long time, angry at him. Why? Why did he go on that bike after he had been drinking? But in the end, I could not stay angry at him. There was no point anymore. I heard that he was buried in another place in Turkey, but where my friend did not know. I could not even pay my last respects to him.

We still went that year to Turkey, but instead of going to Kusadasi, we went to Urkmez. We went one day to the excursion office to see my other friends who worked there, but knowing that I would not see Yilmaz was difficult for me.

I stepped into the office and was greeted by my friend and introduced him to the rest of my family. Of course, Yilmaz came up in conversation, and we talked a bit about him. It was still too hard for me. Before we left and said our goodbyes, he said that he had something for me. He handed me a picture of him sitting at the desk, and next to him stood Yilmaz.

My friend told me that it was the last picture taken of him, and he wanted me to have it. I thanked him and said goodbye.

I will be always grateful to Yilmaz. He saved me the day that I met him. He made sure I was okay and asked nothing in return. Sometimes I forget about him—not because I want to, but as the years go by, it just happens. Writing about him brings me great sadness, but it also brings happy memories back to me. Memories that I will treasure forever. Many other holidays followed, but never like the first one.

He made my holiday alone not alone.

CHAPTER 8
SUICIDE ATTEMPT

Suicide is not a solution.
Help is there when you need it.

IN THIS CHAPTER I WOULD like to take you back to my teenage years when life was not so great for me.

This chapter of my life was difficult to write, but I think it needed to be included in this book, in black and white. I must have been around the age of sixteen or seventeen, possibly even younger than that.

I thought I was doing what everybody else did, just being the teenage kid, but I guess the things that I did were at the wrong time and at the wrong place. Every time I did something that I thought was funny or okay to say or do, it turned out wrong.

In the beginning, I would be told off by whoever, but I could take it and didn't think much of it. But when it started to happen more and more, I started to think that I was not really wanted. I didn't feel wanted by anyone. I just couldn't seem to do anything right. And to make things worse, the normal things in my life started to turn against me too.

With all this going on, I asked myself what my purpose was. What was I still doing here? Did they make a mistake up there by putting me down here, to live this life? As time went on, things did not get any better for me. . . . only, there were no positive thoughts. Happiness was disappearing from my life, replaced by darkness.

Nobody knew how I felt. I was all alone. I just felt I was getting deeper and deeper into this massive black hole that I could not get out of. There was no helping hand, no ladder waiting for me to get me out. No. Instead, there was only more darkness coming in. Tears fell across my face more than once. I could not bear it anymore. I was done with the pain and didn't want to feel the way I felt anymore. I didn't want to be a disappointment to everyone any longer. They would be better off without me.

So, the thought came to me to put an end to my life; after all, nobody would care that I would not be here anymore. I was just in the way. At least, that was my thought process at that time, but I took this very seriously. When I made the decision to end my life, the only question was how.

I decided to find pills or tablets and grab whatever I could to do it that night. I didn't care what kind of pills, as long they would do the trick.

When the night came, I did what I had planned; I got the pills and took them. No second thoughts. I just took them. Somehow, I was glad, thinking everything would be over soon and that I did not have to be here anymore. I know it sounds selfish, but I did not even care about the person who would find me. I did not care about the reaction of my family . . . nothing. I just wanted it to be over and done with and my pain to stop. And with that in mind, I went to sleep.

Morning came, and as I opened my eyes, I realized that I wasn't in the place I wanted to be. I was still here, alive and well. I did not have any side effects from all the different pills I took. I just remember wondering how this was possible. *Why am I still here? Did I not take enough pills? Should I not have died and gone to heaven?* I was mad—mad with life and mad with myself—but could not do anything about it.

Things just carried on from there. I tried to live my life but was never completely happy. Then one day fate changed my path.

I was out with my friend, shopping in the city. I came across a book called *Conversations with God* written by Neal Donald Walsh. When reading the book and understanding what it was about, I related to it. This book became my shield. The shield that helped me battle through the darkness. The author went through the same thing as me, apart from the fact that he never tried to take his own life as I did. He was angry because his life was not going well either. However, instead of taking his anger out on other people, he decided to write a letter to God. He told God about how angry he was, and when he finished the letter, he got an answer back.

I decided there and then to buy the book, and as soon as I had the chance, I read it. I got answers to all my questions reading that book, and when I found out there were more Conversation books, I got them as soon as they came out.

In the end I read all seven books. Those books saved my life. And helped me to start think positively again. I never attempted suicide again.

CHAPTER 9
MEETING DOUGLAS

God works in mysterious ways.

I WILL NOW TELL YOU the story of how I met Douglas, who became my husband.

Douglas and I met on a website. It was not a dating website (although there is nothing wrong with people meeting this way), but funnily enough, it was a multiplayer games site.

I was home with nothing much to do. Usually when that happened, I would play a game on my PC. The game site where I played was pogo.com, where you can play various games, and you have the option to chat with your fellow players playing the same game.

So, while playing the game, I said hello to everybody, wished them good luck, and when they won congratulated them.

At one point in the game, one of the players suggested that we swap photos of each other so we knew who we were talking to. Everybody agreed, and so I sent my photo to all who were in the room.

Little did I know that swapping photos would change my life and start something new. Because immediately after I sent my photo to everybody, I got a private message from someone called *Rockwonder*. I don't remember how the conversation started, but from that moment we became friends, and soon after that we had conversations on MSN.

In our conversations we talked about various things. We spoke about our daily lives and where we lived. When he told me he was from Gibraltar, I had to ask him where the hell that was, as I had never heard of this place.

Although we had just started talking and knew few things about each other, Douglas told me that he liked me as more than just a friend. When he told me that, I held back my feelings and told him that I wasn't sure if I felt the same way back. Despite that, we kept on talking to each other, and the more we did, the more I too started to feel more than friendship for him.

So, slowly but surely, we developed our relationship. We even started to have webcam conversations. I remember once, when I was chatting with him, I went to my kitchen to get a drink, and when coming back to my living room my belly was itchy, so I scratched it.

When I sat back at my PC, he told me not to do that. He told me that lifting my shirt and seeing my stomach gave him goose bumps—in a good way, I guess.

I could not help but start laughing at that comment and explained that it was itchy, nothing more. But from that moment on, every time I went to do something and came back to the room, I lifted my shirt a bit up on purpose, and every time he told me not to do that.

While we had the webcam on, sometimes there were other people in the house, but the one who I saw the most on screen, from a distance, was his father. We never talked with the webcam on as I had learned that his father did not know that he was gay, and he also was still married to his now ex-wife. He told me that when his dad asked about who I was, he told him I was just a friend, so I went along with that.

One day during a phone call with him, things could have been over before they even began. He called to wish me a happy birthday, and during that conversation, something we talked about (I don't remember the details) led to an argument, and I hung up on him. After that conversation

I could only cry. It was my birthday, and what should have been a nice day for me turned into a bad one. We did not speak on MSN or on the phone for three days. But after the three days I called him, and we talked about it and made up.

As we got to know each other better and better through the internet and talking on the phone, the subject of meeting each other for the very first time in person came up. At the time, it was impossible for me to go there. He would have to come to me.

It was a couple of weeks before Christmas when he came over. I could not go to the airport, so I waited at home. He thought that was a bit of a shame, but in the end, he was okay with it. I remember feeling nervous while waiting for him, and when the taxi stopped in front of my door, knowing that it was him, my heart was beating fast. He knocked on the door, and there he was, standing with his back to me. When he turned around, he had red roses in his hand and gave me a kiss and hugged me.

He only stayed with me for a weekend, but he came to see me again just after the New Year and stayed for a week. He met some of my family during that visit. In the week that he was with me, we talked about many things. One of the conversations was about my trip to Morocco. I showed him a photo that I took of an island while on the ferry to Tangiers. He told me that it was Gibraltar.

After a week, it was time to say goodbye again. Saying goodbye was not easy. The first time was hard, but the second time was even harder.

We were back to chatting online and having phone calls, and this time in our conversations we talked about moving in together, but the question was where. He told me that he would come over and live with me. However, I could not let him do that because he had a daughter and a son, who were still very young. So, I decided to go and live in Gibraltar. I did tell him, though, that as soon as he retired, we would go back to live in Amsterdam, which he agreed to.

I did not move straightaway. I thought it was important that he tell his ex-wife first about his sexuality and that he had met me. I felt she had the right to know.

I also wanted to know that we had a place to live together. After he told his ex-wife and found us a home in Spain, I made my travel plans to go over and start a new life with him together, February 8, 2003.

CHAPTER 10
A WHOLE NEW WORLD

A new chapter in a place I'd never heard of before.

THIS WAS IT . . .

A new journey had begun for me. I had just left my country to be with a man I met a couple of months ago.

As I walked through the doors at arrivals, Douglas was there waiting for me. We said hello to each other and hugged. He took my suitcase, and we walked to the exit at Malaga airport to the car park.

We got in the car, where I met his female friend and her daughter, and after saying hello, we made our way to my new home in Spain.

Douglas and I sat in the back holding hands like two teenagers, and couldn't stop looking at each other. When I did have the time to take my eyes away from him because his friend was asking him something, I looked out the window at the strange country I had landed in. Although I knew Spain existed, it was a whole new world for me.

The car ride seemed to last forever, but we finally got to our new home in a place called La Linea de la Concepcion, Cadiz.

We said goodbye to his friends and then went up the stairwell to the front door, which was located at the very top of the building. Once inside, I noticed straightaway that we just had the basic furniture, but that did not bother me whatsoever. After having a look around, we sat on the sofa and had something to drink.

I called my family to say that I was safe and well and that I had already arrived at my new home.

After that I think I fell asleep for a bit. I must have been exhausted from all the excitement, plus the early-morning flight. After my little nap we just talked for the rest of the day and enjoyed each other's company.

The next morning, we went to Gibraltar, the place I now had heard of but had never seen except from the ferry. The first thing I saw getting closer to the border was this huge rock that nobody could miss. I learned that it was called the Rock of Gibraltar. Once through the border, he drove me all around Gibraltar and went up to see the apes who roam freely there.

Everything was new for me, and I must have asked him a thousand and one questions.

After a couple days of living in Spain and going almost every day to Gibraltar, it was time to meet some of his family members. He had arranged for me to meet his sister, Lina, and we would meet her at his kids' school.

So, it was a double meeting, really, but first I met his sister, who was waiting outside the school gates. She knew about Douglas and me as he had told her a long time ago that he was gay.

Meeting Lina was great. We liked each other straightaway. She was very friendly and supportive of me and accepted me with open arms. Now it was time to meet his children, who did not know anything about our relationship. We decided to say I was a friend of his. Meeting his children was very short as they went with his sister to her place. So, basically, it was a quick hello, and that was it, really.

Apart from getting to know his sister and his kids, I also had to get used to other things. Gibraltar was a very small and small-minded country, and everybody knew each other's business, and every time something happened, everyone knew about it. So, when I came to Gibraltar, we were the talk all over town and who knows where else. Personally, it did not affect me, and I didn't give a shit what the people thought of me. I did not know them, and they did not know me, and if I was able to keep it that way, I would have been fine with it. After all, I came from a country where being gay, lesbian, straight or whatever was normal and accepted.

But here it was another story. I was told that a lot of people kept their sexuality secret and it was not to be talked about. Sometimes I had a bit of fun with it, especially when we had a drink somewhere and people were looking at us.

I would tell him to put his house keys behind him, and while the person was looking at us, I would get his keys and purposely touch his butt area while looking back at them. The looks that we got . . . well, I can only say I enjoyed doing it every time.

It was not till much later that everything changed and they accepted same-sex partnership and allowed a civil partnership or marriage.

Come to think of it, yes, I had to get used to some things in this new place, but I guess they had to get more used to me.

CHAPTER 11
THE FIRE

A perfect day can go up in smoke.

IT WAS 10 SEPTEMBER 2003. We had been living in Spain for a couple of months. It was early morning, and we were getting ready to celebrate National Day.

According to Wikipedia,

> The day commemorates Gibraltar's first sovereignty referendum of 1967, in which Gibraltarian voters were asked whether they wished either to pass under Spanish sovereignty or remain under British sovereignty, with institutions of self-government.

They decided or voted to remain under British sovereignty, and they celebrate it every year with street parties, etc. They dress up in the colors of their flag, which are red and white. It's a great event to experience if you ever go and visit.

That morning I went to have a shower but never made it. As I passed by our front door, I noticed smoke, although at that point I did not know it was smoke. I asked Douglas, "What is this?" and he came to look. At that moment I decided to open the front door, which was the worst thing I could have done. As soon as I did, a big massive cloud of black smoke entered our home.

Realizing what it was and what was happening, we closed our front door immediately, but the black smoke had already entered. We were stuck. We were living on the top floor, so we had nowhere to turn. We opened our terrace door to get fresh air and tried to get out that way. But it was too high, and we did not want to fall. We stayed on our terrace, where we could at least breathe, until the fire department arrived. When they had everything almost under control, we were escorted out of the building and to safety.

We both stood outside completely covered in black smoke, waiting to get the all clear to go back up. We heard that a motorcycle parked inside the block on the bottom floor by our neighbor caused the fire. Somehow it caught on fire and exploded, spreading to the main power supply that was also on the bottom floor. As the smoke had nowhere to go, it went up. The smoke lingered at our front door and accumulated there. No wonder it invaded our home so quickly, even though I only opened the door for a second.

When we were given the all clear, we went back upstairs and checked the damage to our home. Everything was covered with soot, from our furniture to the walls—just everything. We left after checking our home and then made our way to Gibraltar. We went to Douglas's father's house where we both had a shower and then still managed to celebrate National Day.

That night, we stayed there to sleep, which was a bit weird and uncomfortable. Douglas slept in his father's room and I slept on the couch. The next morning, Douglas told me his father was concerned I might be uncomfortable sleeping on the couch and kept asking Douglas if I was warm enough and needed an extra blanket.

That day I began to look at him as a very caring man. His father knew by then that we were a couple, but did not like seeing us together. He was an old-fashioned guy and believed in a marriage between a man and a woman. Despite that, he accepted that his son was gay, but for me it still felt weird. We both respected his traditional views, but the night we stayed there, things changed. He accepted me into the family. On many occasions when we went to visit him, he would ask me to help water the plants, and we enjoyed some great conversations, and I finally had the opportunity to get to know my future father-in-law.

The next day we returned to our home and started the big cleanup. At one point during one of the cleaning days, it got to be too much for me, and I sneaked out of our home and went down to the street. I sat at the little square, where I broke down and cried. The owner of the house we rented found me and reassured me that everything would be okay; then he walked me home. After having a talk with Douglas, who was concerned, we continued cleaning the house.

We still had no power and could not stay in our home. We did not want to stay with his father again. Because we wanted our independence, we stayed a couple of days in a house that belonged to one of our landlord's family members, who was away on holiday. When everything was cleaned, and the power was back on, we moved back home. We had a lucky escape, as things could have been far worse.

CHAPTER 12
FINDING WORK

Changes happen, sometimes bad but sometimes good.

AFTER A YEAR OF GETTING used to living in a new country, it was time to find work.

So, I started looking in newspapers to see what kind of jobs were available. I wanted to do the same thing that I did back in Amsterdam, which was helping people with learning disabilities and challenging behaviors. To start, I did not mind doing any odd job I could while working towards where I wanted to be.

Finding work was more difficult than I thought; you had to have qualifications for almost everything. But Douglas knew someone who worked in the disabilities sector, and together we went to meet them.

I took my work experience certificates to the meeting; however, even though she was impressed, there was no work at the time. She was kind enough to keep an eye out and let me know if something came up. After a couple of weeks, there was a vacancy in a job working with children. I applied for the job and was hired on an on-call basis. I took on every shift they offered me so that they saw I was willing to work. I did not want to risk missing out on work and not receiving any more calls.

When I started, I had to shadow other staff members to see how they worked with the clients, and then I would be on my own.

The children who we worked with were spread over several houses. I was lucky enough to spend a long time in one of the children's houses before I moved to two other houses. Working in the two other houses was okay, but most of the time you were stuck in the house due to various things that I of course can't mention.

After working for a year with children, things kind of stopped as there was not so much work for me. Also, I started to not like working with children. I kept with it, but in the meantime, I looked for other jobs. There was nothing until I finally got the opportunity to work in the adult section, so I went for an interview and was successful, but, again, as supply.

We had an induction for a week, and then I went along with a group of eleven others who were also successful to start a period of shadowing other staff members. After a month of getting to know our clients better, we started to work on our own.

Although I was a supply staff member, I was put on a fixed rota, which meant that I had set days that I came in to work. This was good because I did not have to wait until I was called like in the children section.

And if I was called, it was to do an extra shift, which I always said yes to. Where I worked, they had different flats, but I was eventually based in one, while the others were spread between all the other flats.

I soon had only one client that I worked with. I guess that was because there were not many staff members who could work with this person.

When I started to work with this person, we did not have the best connection. After hard work and getting to know each other, we created a very good bond between us. I am proud to say that I contributed to his learning to speak more and learning new words to have better communication. While continuing to improve his vocabulary, I started to do other activities with this person as well.

I would go on walks with him outside, and if the weather was bad, he did his exercises inside. Apart from that, we did guessing games, painting, etc.

He was and is still very clever because he knew that if he did not do his activities, he would not get what he wanted, which was to listen to his music and dance. So, he always did his activities in order to have his music on. I must admit that he became one of my favorites to work with. But when he moved to the UK, I was still working in the same flat with other clients who were great to work with.

Things started to change; the staff that I started with left and new staff came in. I was already a permanent staff member by that time and had been working for eleven years in the same flat. I wanted a change and asked to be moved to another flat.

When this was granted, I was relieved. The change would do me a world of good, and even better, I was going to be working with an old staff member. There were some issues in the beginning, but after having talked about it with each other, things started to look up and we started to work better as a team.

When everything seemed to finally go right, things started to get bad again. Not with the person I was working with, but with our new unit managers.

As this is private and confidential, I can't tell you what happened. The only thing I can tell you is that I went through a period of hell and thought that I was going to lose my job after so many years. Things got so bad that while I was on leave, I was told that I was moved to another flat.

Off course, I was not happy about this. I was not even given a reason why I was moved, at least not until I spoke with human resources. They told me that my skillset would be beneficial in this flat. I was still not happy with this and told them that if I had to be moved to put me back in the very first flat where I started.

In the end we came to an understanding. I would try to work for three months in this flat, and if I was not happy, I could return to the flat I started in. They accepted that. So, against my will I started to work in the new flat and tried to make it work. No matter how much I tried in the beginning, it did not work for me. I even got sick working there. I knew it was not the place for me, but I did the three months as promised. When they were over, I had another conversation with human resources and told them I still wanted to go back to the very first flat I started in. They accepted what I wanted, and I just had to wait for a date to go back. In the meantime, I stayed working in the flat I was in and informed the unit manager myself about me leaving. When I told him, he accepted my decision but said that I was making a mistake. At that time I still knew or thought it was the best decision for me.

But then things changed. I started to feel more comfortable and part of the team and doubted if I really wanted to go back to where I started.

One day I went with another staff member to get the van to go to the villa where we were staying for the summer. My general manager stopped me and asked about writing a letter for me to go back to the old flat. Without hesitation, I said no, it wasn't needed anymore, and said I was going to stay where I was. When the other staff member and I were in the van and driving away, he asked me if I was leaving them. His question made me know for sure that I would stay with them.

I can tell you it was the best decision I ever made. I could not have been happier to be working in that flat with great people who became great friends. I worked there for over three years with great pleasure until it was time for me to return home.

CHAPTER 13
LOSING LINA

You passed away but live in our memories.

THIS CHAPTER WAS A DIFFICULT one for me to write. Difficult because of the way things happened to Douglas's sister, Lina. Although she was not my sister by blood, she felt like one. Lina had medical issues but nothing major apart from having a pacemaker. After she got the pacemaker everything was fine, and she could basically enjoy life again.

In 2009, Douglas and I went on our annual holiday to Amsterdam. While we were there he spoke regularly with Lina and all was fine. One day he had a phone call from one of Lina's friend to advise him that she had been admitted into hospital in Gibraltar due to ear problems.

He called Lina on her mobile to find out what was going on. It seemed that her chronic ear infection had come back and was causing massive headaches. She kept this a secret so as not to spoil our holiday. The following day he spoke with her again, and it seemed that the ear infection had caused a brain abscess. They were planning to transfer her to a Cadiz hospital for further investigation and to start treatment that same day. In Cadiz they did further scans, and they decided to put her on antibiotics for a couple of days.

By then we decided to cancel the rest of the holiday and go back. She said there was no need for that. We spoke over the phone to the neurologist in charge, and he assured us that after a couple of days with antibiotics she would be fine, and she would be back in Gibraltar by then. That evening, she was admitted into one of the wards to start treatment. Unfortunately, that same evening she suffered a seizure due to the rupture of the abscess and had to be put into an induced coma. We only found that out when we called the following morning to speak to her. At that point there was no question about ending our holiday, and as soon as we could, we flew back to Gibraltar, and from there we got the car and drove to Cadiz.

After checking on Lina, we had to sort out a hotel. When we sorted that out, we went back to the hospital and spent time there with her. The doctor spoke to us and said that she would need to have an operation to remove the puss that had accumulated in the brain. The operation would not be without risk, but leaving her like that was also risky.

Douglas needed to give consent, and of course he decided to let them do the operation as there was at least the chance of recovery. The operation lasted for three hours, and when the surgeon came out, he told us that it went well and that they had removed most of it. Now it was a matter of waiting to see how she reacted to the surgery. They tried to take her off the medication so that she would come around, but she was not responding. The days went by, and we went in every day to visit her.

One day I woke up with a good feeling that everything was going to be all right, but boy was I wrong. That morning during breakfast we got a phone call from the doctor who told us to come as soon as possible. Of course, this worried us, and we left the breakfast place without paying. The workers knew us by then and let us pay later. We crossed the street and rushed into the hospital. There the doctor took us into his office and told us that we just missed her and that she passed away.

We both broke down and started crying. We wanted to see her, and the moment that we did, I froze. I could not move. I could only cry.

Douglas cried as well, and I remember him saying to her "Please wake up" a couple of times. Lina was only forty-seven years old.

He gave her a kiss—something I could not do. I was still frozen standing there, not able to move.

It was time to call the family and tell them that she had passed away. I called my family to let them know, and after that we went back to the hotel. I only remember that the same day, family and friends came to be with us, and we went back to Gibraltar. There we arranged the funeral and waited for our sister, Lina, to be brought back to Gibraltar so we could lay her to rest.

When we arrived at the church, it was packed, which was understandable as a lot of people knew her and wanted to pay their last respects. After the service we went home and tried to pick up our lives without her.

Lina was still a young woman with many years left to live. Her life was cut short. She was about to retire so she could enjoy life. Although she is not here anymore, somehow she is watching over us, protecting us, and most of all loving us.

Farewell, dear sister, till we meet again.

CHAPTER 14
GOING HOME ON VACATION

Doubts are always there; you must set them to rest.

WHEN I STARTED LIVING IN Gibraltar, I would go back for vacations to Amsterdam, my home city. The first time I returned was after three months in Gibraltar. Of course, I was happy to visit, but returning to Gibraltar was another story.

It was nice to see family and friends again. It was great. We had a lot to catch up on. We talked about things that had happened since I'd been away and, of course, what I had been doing in Gibraltar and how things were different for me there.

When it was time to go back to Gibraltar, I thought I would be fine.

Saying goodbye was difficult. It felt almost like the first time when I left to start my journey. The sadness started during the flight. I remember feeling down and not talking much. When we got back to Gibraltar, my mood changed even more, and for the first week Douglas was not able to talk to me. I did not want to talk. I don't even know why, really, but it happened. After a week I was fine, and I just carried on with my daily life.

On our next vacation to Amsterdam, everything was fine until we returned, and the same thing started to happen. Again, I did not want to talk, and this also took another week to get over. I started to wonder what was happening and why. *Did I make a mistake? Should I have left my country? My family and friends? Should I never have started this journey?* All these questions went through my head, and I could not make any sense of it.

As I did not really know what to do, I just left it. But when it happened for a third time, I could not ignore it anymore, as it was not fair on Douglas to deal with this every time we returned.

I had questions to answer for myself and decisions to make. After thinking about it for couple of days, I decided that I did make the right decision. I made the right choice to follow my heart, although that was not the solution to all my problems.

So, I decided that I had to change my way of thinking next time I visited my family and friends in Amsterdam. I would be more okay with going back Gibraltar. I say more okay—I had to take baby steps and work to improve my mindset with time. Slowly but surely things started to get better for me, knowing that the next time I went back to Gibraltar I would be more okay with it. With time, my ability to handle it improved.

At one point, I did not even think about it anymore, and it just became a normal thing for me. I was over it. It took me a while, but I did it.

It wasn't until many years later, after returning from our regular vacation to Amsterdam, that it happened again. The same feeling of sadness returned. It scared me and I started to panic. But luckily this time it did not last. In fact, the feeling went away all by itself. After that, my holidays coming and going back were fine. In fact, the person who had more trouble with it now was Douglas.

It is strange to me how things turned out. But don't get me wrong: every time I fly above Amsterdam, I take a deep breath, relieved that I am back to visit again.

CHAPTER 15
THE WEDDING DAY

You showed me your love and I said yes.

GETTING MARRIED WAS SOMETHING I never wanted to do. I believe you don't need a piece of paper to say that you love each other. I understand that for some people it is important, and that was the case for Douglas.

When we first got together, I was not even thinking about marriage, and at that point there was still no same-sex marriage in Gibraltar. So, for many years I did not think or speak about it with Douglas. When it did come up in conversations, I told him that I did not want to get married and said, as I stated before, that I didn't need a piece of paper to say that I loved someone.

But when the law changed, and they accepted same-sex civil partnerships, which is basically the same as a marriage, Douglas wanted to get married. I had to respect what he wanted too; after all, it was not only me in this relationship. At that point I think I was more ready to plan our civil partnership.

When we set a date for the sixth of October, we had only six months.

Six months was really a short time to arrange everything, but we managed to do it. First, we had to make a guest list, and we both decided that we did not want a big group of people. We had to be selective in who we were going to invite. In the end it came to seventy or eighty people who would share our special day with us. We also had to do the invitations. Luckily, we both liked the same design for them. We ordered them, and as soon as we had them, we sent them out quickly due to our short timeline. After that, we sorted out the rest, like our rings, suits, wedding venue, etc. Everything went well and smoothly. We never had a problem or disagreements about anything, which is always a bonus. As the date came closer, we had everything almost sorted and had time to relax and to take it all in and enjoy ourselves a bit.

We spent time with my sisters and my sisters' friend at the time, who came over to be with us on our special day. I was glad; I thought I would have no family here and would just have the friends that I made here.

The big day arrived. Soon I would be a married man. Strangely enough, I was not nervous. I was only nervous about correctly repeating what the ceremony master wanted me to say. I feared messing up. Funnily enough, it was not me who messed up the words a bit. Douglas did, which we both laughed at. After the ceremony, that was it. I was a married man—well, at that point, in a civil partnership. While the guests made their way to the venue, we went to Commonwealth Park for our wedding pictures, but when we arrived, our photographer was nowhere to be seen. It turned out that he was still doing another job but would soon be on his way. We had to wait at least an hour for him to arrive. In that time, I thought of just taking some photos of us together with a mobile phone, but no; we waited for the photographer.

In the meantime, our guests arrived at the venue, but as we were still waiting to have our wedding photos taken, they had to wait. When we had done the photos, we made our way to the venue, which was close by. We welcomed everyone in and gave them a welcoming drink as we had planned. Another special touch we arranged was that every person had a lilac rose on their plate.

After we had eaten, the party could finally start. My plan was to get drunk, but it did not matter how much I drank or mixed my drinks; I was unable to get drunk. I was a bit disappointed about that, but some of the guests managed to get drunk—and Douglas!

In the end, it was a great day and night that lasted into the early morning . . . which was not so great as we had our flight early the following day. We did not sleep and drank coffee to stay awake and waited to be picked up to go to Malaga airport for our flight to Florence.

When we arrived there, we had been awake for more than twenty-four hours. After checking in, we both went to the hotel room and fell asleep. We went out later that evening to eat something, and then returned to our room to rest up further as we were still tired.

The next couple of days we spent sightseeing before moving on to our next destination, which was Venice. When we arrived in Venice, we were picked up in a car, and while driving to our hotel we were both surprised not to see any water. That was a bit of a disappointment, but that changed when we arrived at the place where we had to get the boat to our hotel. It was suddenly a whole other world. It felt like we stepped out of reality and into a fantasy world.

It was an amazing experience, but I must say it was also expensive there. I guess that's why we did not do as many excursions there as in Florence. But we saw the most famous landmarks. After our few days in Venice, it was time to go to our last destination, my hometown of Amsterdam. In Amsterdam we just chilled out and did whatever we wanted to do. We planned a big party to celebrate our wedding with family who could not come over or make it to be with us on the big day. From there we flew back and continued our normal daily routine, only this time as a married couple.

Soon we will be celebrating our fifth wedding anniversary. After almost five years, Gibraltar made it possible to convert your civil partnership into marriage. Which we of course did. So, my last words in this chapter are for my hubby:

Thank you for being a part of my life and thank you for loving me the way you do. Here's to many more years together.

I love you.

CHAPTER 16
A SPIRITUAL JOURNEY

You are a spiritual being. You must simply tap into it.

MY SPIRITUAL JOURNEY STARTED YEARS and years ago. Way before I met Douglas and before I left Amsterdam. What I did not know was that I would continue this spiritual journey here in Gibraltar. So, let me take you back to how it all began.

When I was still living in Amsterdam, I went out a lot with my best friend to the city. One day we went into a shop, and while walking around I saw a pack of tarot cards and figured I would buy it and see how it went. The first time I tried it, I followed the instructions, which tell you to lay all the cards out and bless them. I began by doing readings for myself. I asked a question while shuffling the cards and then laid them out. As I had no previous knowledge of what the cards meant, I used the booklet that explained what every card meant and represented.

My first attempt was not very helpful, but for some reason I kept on trying it. And things started to come out of it; the explanation made sense to me. My interest grew and grew, so I started to get more into it and tried not to use the explanation booklet. I started to use my own interpretations, and with time I got better at it. I decided that I wanted to continue with this and develop it more.

So, I started with baby steps by doing readings for my family. I did it for them first because if I got the reading wrong, it wouldn't matter because my family would not judge me. And they knew I was just starting.

Of course, not every reading that I did for my family went right, but slowly the readings became better, and before I knew it, my family wanted more readings from me. One reading that always stayed with me was one I did for my brother-in-law. I told him something was going to happen with his car, and eight months later it did. I don't remember what exactly happened.

During this time, I also started to go to regular spiritual evenings, where you could put down an object or photo on the table, and if you were lucky enough to be picked out, the medium would tell things about you. I was not always picked, and that did not really matter for me. I was quite happy to just hear all the wonderful stories, which often turned out to be true for that person. During my time going there I was picked out several times.

Not all the mediums who came there turned out to be great. I went one time with one of my sisters who also liked those evenings, but this evening there were three mediums doing readings. And each of them did something different: one with photos, one for animals, and the third one did something else. The one who did the animals was terrible. She picked out a photo of somebody's cat and started to talk about the cat. When she asked whose photo it was, a woman put up her hand. So, the medium talked a bit more about the cat, but in the present sense. But the cat's owner told her that the cat had passed away. The medium responded, "Oh, well, let's see where she is and if I can find her."

My sister and I both looked at each other. Was she serious? It was quiet for a while—so quiet that you could hear a motorcycle going by, and when that happened my sister just said out of the blue, "Look, there he goes." I had to hold my laughter, and I think I was not the only one. Luckily, she was not told off, and I can tell you at the end the medium could not find the cat.

But, generally, there were great mediums who came there and gave excellent readings. Like I said before, I was picked out several times, and one of the last times I was picked out, the woman told me I was going to move. I told her that I did not have any intentions to move, but she kept on saying it.

At that point I thought, *Yeah, okay*, but then when I met Douglas, I did move, so at the end of the day she was right.

When I moved to Gibraltar, I took my trusty tarot cards with me, and after settling into my new life, I started to do some tarot readings again. I even created a website where people could ask questions and I would do the reading for them and send it. The feedback I received was always good, but after a while I stopped doing readings—not because they went wrong or anything. It was just time for me to move on and take the next step of my spiritual journey.

That step happened when I was still working with children. There I met a new colleague called Marie with whom I became friends. When talking to her during a night shift, I found out that we had a lot in common, and one of those things was spirituality. I learned that she was a Reiki master teacher and apart from that was able to see and hear things.

She told me that I would be good at giving Reiki, and with that, I started to learn the basics of Reiki healing. One of the key elements was to learn to meditate, which in the beginning did not work well for me. I could not switch off my thoughts during meditation. But when I started to meditate more and more, my meditations started to get better, and I started to see things, beginning with colors.

Not only did I start meditations, I also had a course book to read and had to learn symbols. And on top of all that, Marie wanted me to answer a question before we could move on.

I cannot tell you what my answer to her question was; that part is for every person to find out if they ever start a Reiki course. But I can tell you that it was the correct answer. It was the answer she wanted to hear. So, after I received my attunement, I got my certificate stating I was now a Reiki One practitioner.

Soon after I had done my Reiki One, I started with Reiki Two, which was similar but also different. I had to get used to new music, etc., during the Reiki Two course. She told me that I would become a Reiki master teacher just like her, but I told her that I was happy with passing Reiki Two and that was enough.

Well, three years after I started, I became a Reiki master teacher, which meant that I was able to teach others in the wonderful art of Reiki. It was a very strange and surreal thing for me to think that I was a teacher and that I would have students. After coming around to the whole idea, I started to promote myself online and advertise Reiki One classes. I had no clue how things would go and how I would conduct my classes. But I decided to run the classes or course the same as I had learned them.

My next question was whether I would get students who were really interested in it. But soon after I advertised, I started to get responses from people. Soon I had my very first student that I would teach Reiki.

I must admit that when I started with my very first student, I was nervous and hoped that everything would turn out well. I was this time telling a student what to do. And would I know the answers to their questions?

Luckily, everything went well, and it was a pleasure having her as my very first student. She was grateful and even made me a positive box as a gift. Since then I have had more students who passed their Reiki courses with me, and to this day, I am still giving courses in various grades of Reiki.

In Reiki, students choose who they want as their Reiki master teacher. For me it is an honor that people want to be taught by me. Furthermore, not only am I helping them, but also they are helping me to grow in my spiritual journey.

CHAPTER 17
BECOMING AN AUTHOR

Discover your potential and you may be surprised.

I NEVER THOUGHT OF BECOMING an author because let's face it—me, writing a book? Me?

I like reading books that get my attention, but writing a book myself was never something I thought about. It was not until recently that I decided I wanted to put my quotes and sayings in a booklet or book form.

I started writing quotes and sayings that came to me from above. Yes, from above; I always listen to my feelings and never write a quote or saying without getting the inspiration.

Whenever I wrote one down, I posted it on a famous page and continued doing this for a while. I then decided to make my own page and post them there for more people to see and to enjoy. I was curious to see how other people would react to them. And when people started to comment on my quotes and sayings and liking my page that I created, I posted more and more of them. Reading all the comments showing that people could relate to them made me think.

It made me think of writing a book. A book with my quotes and sayings. But as I had no clue where or how to start the process, I decided to look for a publisher online. I also posted on a famous website that I was looking for a publisher. At first, I had no reply, but when I posted it again a couple of days later, I got a reply in the first couple of hours. The guy who replied to me worked and is still working for a famous company that publishes books. After some messages back and forward, we set a time to meet each other.

The day that we met, we talked about how the process worked, what they needed from me, and what kind of cover I would like, etc. He also asked to see some of the quotes and sayings I wrote, which I had prepared for him.

After our meeting, I kept in contact with this person to discuss things further and learn the cost involved. But the cost apparently depends on how many copies you want them to print. When I got the print prices by email, I discussed this with Douglas. Was I willing to pay a big amount so I could have my book published? Would anyone really buy it?

So, after discussing everything, I had doubts. I did not stop the process but rather prolonged it. Then a friend of ours, Rosanna, told me about self-publishing and sent me the details by email. I checked it out and everything looked straightforward. And the best thing was that you did not have to pay anything.

The only thing was that when you get paid for the number of books you have sold, the self-publishing platform takes a percentage.

I thanked her for the help, but then she told me she would like to help me further as she used to be an editor. I just had to wait a couple of weeks for her to come over from Australia, and when she did, together with Douglas we went through the manuscript and started to get everything ready.

When it was all done, I was ready to publish my very first book online. Oh my god, it was now up for sale—my quotes and sayings. My book called *Healing Messages from Above.*

I was a bit nervous about how people would react but at the same time excited. I suddenly was an author. The funny thing is that I forgot to put two or three quotes in that book, and both Douglas and Rosanna said, "Well, you can put those in your next book."

I had to laugh and say no thank you. I just wanted to write a book one time, and that was enough. But a couple of months later, I started to write this book. It may not have many chapters, but, hey, I am still new to all this, and I felt that I had to write this book and publish it online again—maybe even really publish it this time.

In the meantime, I started to write new quotes and sayings that I published on my page. I don't have many now, but who knows; when I have enough of them, I may publish another book. We never know what is waiting for us.

CHAPTER 18
STAY OR GO BACK HOME?

Year by year waiting to go, until the unexpected happened.

RETURNING HOME.

Gosh, words that I thought I would never say.

But yes, it's happening. I am going back to Amsterdam to live again in my home country.

I am so looking forward to it, but it also feels weird to go back. Weird because I've got mixed feelings. I don't even know how to describe it.

After all, I have lived in Gibraltar for about seventeen years. There are so many things that have happened here, so many memories, so many things that people don't know about. That's why I will always think of it as my second home.

It was always in our plans to go back to Amsterdam as soon as Douglas retired. Or I would go without him, I always joked. I am happy to say he still wants to come with me. And now that the time has nearly come, we are making our plans to go over and start the rest of our lives there. We are looking for a house, but we will only be looking, for the moment—until we are closer to going.

Right now I am still focused on our lives here as that doesn't stop. When the time comes, I will be ready to settle over there. We will come back often to Gibraltar to see how everything is with our house here and to see our family and friends.

Returning home will be like starting all over again; although I am from there, it still feels like that. I've been back to my home country many times, but that was only for holidays. Now I am going to be living there again. Starting again. Making a new life again. Our first year back over there will be spent just enjoying things like going on mini holidays back to Gibraltar and taking it easy.

After that, we both want to find a twenty-hour job to basically keep some money coming in. I would really like to start something for myself, start my own business, but I just have to wait and see. If that is not possible, I can look for a job in care as I have enough experience in this field. And Douglas hopefully will find something that he likes doing as well.

A few months away from moving, with reality setting in, I' started to question myself. I asked myself, *After all these years living away from my home country, will I be able to live there again?* The very thought scared me. *Can I? What if it does not work out? What to do then? Will I go back to Gibraltar?* I had no answers to these questions. The days went by, and I still had that very unsettled feeling.

I knew that I needed to talk about it with Douglas and see what he thought. I was not looking forward to the conversation as I knew how much he is looking forward to the move. One day while having lunch I asked him, "What if we can't find a house in Amsterdam?"

His answer was simple: "Then we stay in Gibraltar." He continued, "I am going to tell you one thing, if we do move to Amsterdam to live, you will be wanting to come back to Gibraltar sooner than I would."

I was really surprised. I thought he would react differently. I guess that teaches me not to judge someone or, like I always say, to think for them.

I felt relieved with his answer. It was like a weight lifting off my shoulders. We discussed it a bit further and even discussed doing six months here and six months back over in Amsterdam. With all this said, we had a holiday coming up to Amsterdam, and I decided to see how I felt, starting with a very simple thing I always do on the approach.

When flying above Amsterdam, I always take a deep breath and think, *I'm back in my home country*, and it always gives me a good feeling. When I did it this time, it was not the same, and I had to do it a few times to get the same feeling. After that, I was fine. I enjoyed spending time with family and friends—until the conversation came up. Even after having talked about it with Douglas and deciding what we were going to do, it still got to me. At one point I really started to get overwhelmed and stressed by it. It almost felt like a panic attack.

Once again, I talked to Douglas about it, and he calmed me down by saying that we would do what we wanted. I guess that it all became too much for me at that point, thinking about how everybody was looking forward to seeing me back in Amsterdam again after all these years living abroad, but still struggling with the question of whether I still wanted that.

Now I feel better when talking about it and have gotten some little things already sorted. I am even looking forward to it a little more. How everything will go, I don't know. Only time will tell.

CHAPTER 19
THE VOICE OF SELF-DOUBT

A battle I had to fight alone.
Here I am again.

A VOICE FROM THE PAST spoke to me, and sounded so familiar. A voice that I had not heard for a long time. A voice I thought I got rid of. It was back. The doubt instantly struck, with panicked thoughts going through my head.

Thoughts about whether I was doing the right thing. Thoughts that told me I was not strong enough. *NO, stop!* I yelled in my mind. Why did this voice come back to haunt me? I had no time to think. Its return took me back to past events playing in my head like a movie. While looking at it all I asked myself, *Should I have spoken up at that moment or stayed silent like I did?*

Through the years I learned to live with the voice within, and soon it fell into the background, and eventually it stopped. I learned to speak my mind, and knew when to keep silent or ignore things. I stood up for myself and argued for things I believed in. Now the voice of doubt was back again, trying to take control.

There have been times it won the battle. On minor things, but it still won. I allowed it to win only to wonder afterwards why I allowed it to win. The voice of doubt is not always there; it likes to surprise me from time to time—most of the time during moments that I would prefer it stay away. It scares me to the point I fall silent and the words I want to say don't come out. I ask myself, *Am I that weak? Don't I have an opinion? Do I agree with what is being said or done?*

When the voice of doubt speaks again, it tells me to give in to it all. For a moment I do, and I let it take me back to the deep dark hole I was in before.

Before it gets the chance to take me there once again, I say *no.* The real me steps up and keeps me out of the darkness. The real me knows the voice of doubt is not strong enough yet to take control of me again. I don't need to go back to the darkness where I was once invisible and nonexistent to everyone and let the voice of doubt win.

I will fight back. I'm fighting back with all my heart. I start by telling myself that I am good enough. I started to love myself all over again and tell myself that I deserve to be loved. Slowly but surely, I build myself up again. I don't see darkness anymore, just a bright light. A bright light that is shining for me, showing me new possibilities that I did not know before or maybe did not want to see. I say what I think again and stand behind it. If I must argue with someone, so be it.

I am doing much better now and am on the road to recovery. The voice of doubt is sometimes still around and tries to get back into my life. I have learned to listen to it and recognize it for what it is. But I have made a new friend in the meantime called the voice of reason, who brings me back to me. He stops me when it is needed. He lets me reason with myself. He tells me that the best advice you can get is from yourself. The voice of reason is me.

ACKNOWLEDGMENTS

First, I would like to thank one of my sisters for filling in some of the blanks for a specific chapter. Without her help that chapter would be incorrect and incomplete. Also, I would like to thank her for encouraging me to write this book.

The next person I would like to thank is my husband, Douglas, for his support and patience during my writing of this book. Thank you for being one of my editors and for your unconditional love.

Next, I would like to thank Rosanna for helping me out with the final touches of this book. Thank you for your patience and for respecting my wishes as this book is very special to me.

And I would like to thank Marie for her support and wise words that I always kept in mind while writing this book.

CPSIA information can be obtained
at www.ICGtesting.com
Printed in the USA
LVHW111648251120
672676LV00004B/56

9 781646 631810